NLP in Business Coaching:

Enhancing Performance and Productivity

By Rex Morton

Copyright Page

Disclaimer

This book is intended to provide information about the fields of Neuro-Linguistic Programming (NLP) and Cognitive Behavioural Therapy (CBT) and their potential integration. While the author has made every effort to ensure that the information was correct at the time of publication, the author does not assume and hereby disclaims any liability to any party for any loss, damage, or disruption caused by errors or omissions, whether such errors or omissions result from negligence, accident, or any other cause.

The contents of this book should not be used as a substitute for professional advice, diagnosis, or treatment. The reader should always consult with a qualified healthcare provider about any mental health concerns or conditions. Never disregard professional psychological or medical advice or delay in seeking it because of something you have read in this book.

The views expressed in this work are solely those of the author and do not necessarily reflect the views of the publisher, and the publisher hereby disclaims any responsibility for them.

The inclusion of websites, links, or references to other resources does not mean that the author or the publisher endorses the information the organization or website may provide or recommendations it might make. Furthermore, the author does not guarantee the accuracy of the information these resources provide.

The use of any information provided in this book is solely at your own risk.

Understanding the Importance of Business Coaching

The corporate landscape is more volatile and challenging than ever before. From startups to established corporations, organizations are constantly on the lookout for strategies and tools that can give them a competitive edge. One such tool is business coaching, a method for moving a company from where it is today to where the owner or staff wants it to be.

Business coaching is an essential leadership tool that can bring about significant improvement in productivity, performance, and profitability. It provides an external perspective to the business operations and offers constructive criticism, fostering a learning environment that encourages continuous improvement. Furthermore, business coaching promotes self-awareness, builds confidence, enhances decision-making skills, and encourages personal development, all of which are essential in the rapidly changing business environment.

Introduction to Neuro-Linguistic Programming (NLP)

A psychological strategy called neuro-linguistic programming (NLP) entails studying the tactics employed by successful people and using them to accomplish personal objectives. It links the ideas, words, and behavior patterns that people develop throughout time to certain results.

In order to enhance the effectiveness and quality of people's lives, NLP focuses on discovering and using thought patterns that affect behavior. Neurology, language, and programming are three facets that are essential to the human experience. The neurological system controls how our bodies work, language defines how we interact with others, and programming dictates the kinds of representations of the world we construct.

How NLP and Business Coaching Intersect

The synergy between NLP and business coaching provides a powerful tool for transformative change within organizations. On one hand, business coaching helps to optimize business processes, improve performance, and enhance leadership skills. On the other, NLP focuses on the internal mental processes, belief systems, and behavioral patterns that drive these aspects.

When combined, NLP empowers business coaching with advanced communication skills, the ability to establish rapid rapport, and methods to model and replicate success. For instance, NLP techniques can be used to help an individual recognize and modify limiting beliefs or negative thought patterns, thereby enhancing their capacity to perform effectively in their business role.

Moreover, NLP can enrich the coach-client relationship by fostering effective communication and understanding. It also offers techniques to embed new, beneficial behaviors and mindsets, leading to sustainable growth and performance improvement.

Objectives and Scope of the Book

This book aims to provide a comprehensive understanding of how Neuro-Linguistic Programming (NLP) can be used in business coaching to enhance performance and productivity. It intends to guide business coaches, leaders, HR professionals, and anyone interested in personal and professional development through the basics of NLP, its practical application in business, and the impact it can create.

The book outlines the core principles and techniques of NLP and delves into how these can be utilized for improving communication, fostering leadership skills, enhancing personal productivity, and driving successful team dynamics. It also explores how NLP can be integrated into business coaching practices and provides real-world case studies illustrating its transformative potential.

By the end of this book, the reader should have a solid grasp of NLP's potential in business coaching and be equipped with practical techniques to leverage it in their professional practice or personal growth journey.

Chapter II: Foundation of Neuro-Linguistic Programming

Historical Background and Development of NLP

Neuro-Linguistic Programming (NLP) was developed in the 1970s by Richard Bandler, a mathematician, and John Grinder, a linguist. Their aim was to discover why certain therapists were more successful than others and to replicate their methods. They studied the work of eminent therapists, such as Fritz Perls, the founder of Gestalt therapy, and Virginia Satir, a renowned family therapist, as well as the innovative linguistic techniques of Alfred Korzybski and Noam Chomsky.

Through their research, Bandler and Grinder developed a range of techniques and methods to guide individuals in enhancing their communication, personal development, and psychotherapy. NLP quickly grew in popularity and has been applied in various fields including business, education, sports, and health.

Principles and Tenets of NLP

NLP is guided by a set of principles and tenets that form its foundation. Some of the fundamental presuppositions of NLP include:

The Map is Not the Territory: Our perception of reality is not reality itself but our own 'map' or interpretation of it. Everyone has their unique way of interpreting the world based on their experiences, beliefs, and values.

The Meaning of Communication is the Response You Get: Communication is deemed successful based on the response it elicits, regardless of the communicator's intention. If a message is not understood, it is the sender's responsibility to alter the message or its delivery.

There is No Failure, Only Feedback: This principle promotes a growth mindset by viewing mistakes not as failures but as learning opportunities.

Mind and Body are Part of the Same System: This tenet emphasizes that our thoughts, feelings, and actions are interconnected, and changes in one can influence the others.

Exploring the Basic Techniques and Methods in NLP

Several techniques and methods underpin the practice of NLP. These include:

Rapport: The process of creating a bond of mutual understanding and trust with another person, often by mirroring their body language, vocal tone, and speech patterns.

Anchoring: Associating a particular sensory experience with a specific emotional state, allowing one to access desired emotions or states at will.

Reframing: Changing the context or perspective of a situation to transform its meaning and influence the emotional response.

Swish Pattern: A technique used to change unwanted behaviors or responses by replacing them with desirable ones.

Meta-Model: A set of questions designed to clarify communication, uncover underlying assumptions, and explore deeper levels of thought.

Scientific Evidence and Case Studies Supporting NLP

While NLP has faced criticism regarding its scientific validity, numerous studies and anecdotal case studies highlight its efficacy in various domains. Research has demonstrated the effectiveness of NLP techniques in improving mental health, interpersonal communication, and performance in sports and business.

Case studies in the business world reveal how NLP has helped improve sales performance, leadership skills, team dynamics, and customer satisfaction. More comprehensive case studies will be discussed later in the book, demonstrating the transformative potential of NLP in business coaching.

Chapter III: NLP and the Mindset Shift in Business

NLP for Personal Development and Mindset Change

NLP is a potent tool for personal development and mindset change, playing a crucial role in transforming an individual's thought patterns and beliefs to optimize performance. By utilizing various techniques, NLP enables individuals to break free from self-imposed constraints, foster resilience, build confidence, and enhance their problem-solving skills.

For example, an executive struggling with public speaking may use the 'Swish Pattern' technique. The executive would visualize the anxiety-provoking scenario of public speaking and then 'swish' this image with a more confident version of themselves delivering a powerful speech. With regular practice, the executive may experience diminished anxiety and increased confidence.

Empowering Beliefs and Overcoming Limiting Beliefs with NLP

Beliefs shape our perception of the world, affecting our decisions, actions, and outcomes. While empowering beliefs propel us towards success, limiting beliefs may hinder growth and achievement. NLP techniques can assist in replacing limiting beliefs with empowering ones.

Consider a business owner who believes that failure is devastating and reflects personal inadequacy. This limiting belief might prevent the owner from taking calculated risks or innovating. An NLP coach could use 'reframing' to shift this mindset. They could encourage the business owner to see failure not as a personal flaw but as a valuable learning opportunity and a stepping stone to success.

NLP for Goal Setting and Vision Creation

NLP offers effective strategies for goal setting and vision creation. It encourages setting 'Well-Formed Outcomes,' goals that are positive, within one's control, sensory-specific, and framed in a way that considers the wider impact on one's life.

Imagine a team leader aiming to improve team productivity. Rather than setting a vague goal like "I want to improve productivity," an NLP-driven goal might be "I want to increase our team's output by 15% in the next quarter, by refining our project management process and promoting proactive communication within the team."

Hypothetical Examples and Hypothetical Case Studies

Hypothetical Case Study: Overcoming Limiting Beliefs: A sales executive harbored the limiting belief that clients were indifferent to her presentations, which affected her performance. Through NLP coaching, she discovered her belief was rooted in a few past experiences rather than the truth. She replaced her limiting belief with a new, empowering one: "I have valuable insights to offer, and my clients are interested in hearing them." Over the next few months, her presentation delivery improved, as did her sales numbers.

Hypothetical Case Study: Goal Setting and Vision Creation: A startup founder struggled to set concrete business goals, leading to a lack of focus and slow progress. With NLP coaching, he learned to set well-formed outcomes, creating a clear vision for his startup. He defined specific, measurable goals that took into account the current state of the business and the resources available. As a result, he and his team were able to make strategic decisions and substantially increase the business's growth rate.

NLP and the Art of Persuasion and Influence

Effective persuasion and influence are critical in the business world, whether it's in sales pitches, team leadership, or stakeholder management. NLP provides techniques to enhance these skills by understanding and utilizing the power of language and non-verbal communication. The 'Meta-Model' in NLP, for example, is a set of language patterns that reveal underlying assumptions, beliefs, and omitted information, thus enabling more persuasive communication.

For instance, a sales representative might use NLP to connect better with customers, uncover their needs, and tailor their product's presentation to match those needs, thus significantly improving their persuasion and influence abilities.

Mirroring, Pacing, and Leading: Enhancing Rapport with NLP

Rapport is the foundation of effective communication, and NLP techniques such as mirroring, pacing, and leading can significantly enhance it. Mirroring involves subtly copying the other person's body language, voice tonality, and words. Pacing means matching the person's emotional state and understanding their viewpoint, while leading involves guiding them towards a new perspective or emotional state.

A manager might use these techniques to build rapport with team members, thereby fostering better communication, trust, and cooperation. For example, if a team member is anxious about a project deadline, the manager could pace by acknowledging the concern, then lead by discussing a plan to tackle the task effectively and reduce the anxiety.

NLP for Conflict Resolution and Negotiation

NLP also offers tools for conflict resolution and negotiation. The key is to understand the other party's perspective deeply (their 'map' of the world) and communicate in a way that resonates with them. Techniques such as 'reframing' can be used to shift viewpoints and find common ground.

Consider a situation where two business partners disagree on their company's growth strategy. An NLP-trained mediator could help each partner understand the other's viewpoint, reframe the disagreement as a mutual search for the best solution, and guide them towards a compromise that respects both perspectives.

Examples and Role-play Scenarios

Example - Persuasion and Influence: An HR executive uses the 'Meta-Model' questions to convince the board of directors about a new employee development program. They uncover the board's underlying assumptions and address those, providing specific, concrete details about the program's benefits and return on investment.

Role-play Scenario - Conflict Resolution: Two team leaders, Alice and Bob, disagree about resource allocation for their projects. An NLP coach, acting as a mediator, could guide a role-play exercise where Alice and Bob each express their viewpoints, mirror and pace each other's perspectives, and then explore potential compromises through reframing.

Through such examples and scenarios, this book aims to equip readers with practical tools to improve their business communication using NLP.

Using NLP for Stress Management and Resilience Building

NLP can be effective in managing stress and building resilience by reframing stressful situations, anchoring positive states, and replacing negative thoughts with positive ones. For instance, an executive under pressure might use the 'Swish Pattern' technique to replace feelings of stress and anxiety with a state of calm and focus. By repeatedly practicing this technique, the executive could build resilience and handle pressure more effectively.

NLP for Boosting Confidence and Leadership Qualities

NLP techniques can also be used to boost confidence and enhance leadership qualities. Visualization, for instance, can help individuals build a mental image of themselves as confident and influential leaders. Leaders can also use mirroring and pacing to build rapport with their teams, inspiring trust and respect.

For example, a team leader who feels apprehensive about leading a new project could visualize herself successfully managing and delivering the project, fostering a sense of confidence and capability.

Enhancing Creativity and Problem-Solving Skills with NLP

NLP can foster creativity and enhance problem-solving skills by reframing problems as opportunities and encouraging flexible thinking. Techniques such as 'Disney Strategy,' a method that involves viewing a problem from three perspectives (dreamer, realist, critic), can significantly improve creative problem solving.

An engineer facing a challenging design problem could use the 'Disney Strategy' to explore a wide range of innovative solutions, assess their feasibility, and refine them to best meet the project requirements.

NLP in Time Management and Productivity

NLP can help improve time management and productivity by shaping perceptions of time and promoting focus and motivation. Techniques such as 'timeline therapy' can help individuals visualize tasks more clearly and manage their time more effectively.

Consider a project manager struggling with project timelines. Through 'timeline therapy,' the manager could visualize the project's timeline, identify potential bottlenecks, and plan accordingly, thus improving their time management and overall project productivity.

Hypothetical Case Studies in Performance Enhancement with NLP

Hypothetical Case Study - Stress Management: A CEO of a start-up was facing high levels of stress due to the multitude of responsibilities. Through NLP coaching, they learned to use the 'Swish Pattern' technique, enabling them to replace stress and overwhelm with feelings of calm and control. As a result, they were able to lead their company more effectively and make sounder decisions.

Hypothetical Case Study - Leadership Development: An aspiring leader lacked the confidence to speak up in meetings. They were coached in using NLP techniques, including visualization and anchoring. They visualized themselves speaking confidently and anchored that feeling to a physical gesture. Over time, this practice significantly boosted their confidence, allowing them to voice their ideas and take on leadership roles.

Hypothetical Case Study - Creativity and Problem Solving: A product development team was stuck on a challenging problem. The team leader introduced the 'Disney Strategy.' The team brainstormed dreamer, realist, and critic perspectives, leading to a breakthrough in their problem-solving approach and an innovative solution.

These hypothetical case studies highlight the transformative potential of NLP in enhancing individual and team performance in a business setting.

Using NLP to Foster Effective Team Communication

NLP can be used to enhance team communication by teaching individuals to understand and respect diverse communication styles and preferences. For example, some team members may be more 'visual' and prefer diagrams and charts, while others may be more 'auditory' or 'kinesthetic,' preferring discussions or hands-on tasks. Recognizing these preferences can improve the clarity and effectiveness of team communication.

Consider a project manager who notices some team members struggle to grasp the project's scope from written briefs. By understanding their preference for auditory or kinesthetic information, the manager might choose to explain the project's details through a discussion or a hands-on workshop, leading to improved understanding and more effective communication within the team.

NLP for Building Trust and Cohesion in Teams

Building trust and cohesion within a team is crucial for productivity and morale. NLP techniques, such as mirroring and pacing, can create a sense of understanding and rapport, while reframing can help resolve conflicts and foster a positive team atmosphere.

Imagine a team with trust issues due to frequent misunderstandings. An NLP coach could conduct a workshop teaching them NLP techniques to understand each other better, build rapport, and address conflicts. Over time, these techniques could significantly improve trust and cohesion within the team.

NLP for Organizational Change and Transformation

NLP can also facilitate organizational change and transformation by shaping perceptions and beliefs about change and encouraging positive attitudes. An organization undergoing a significant transformation might use NLP to reframe the change as an opportunity for growth and improvement rather than a threat.

For instance, a company planning a major digital transformation could use NLP techniques to address employee fears and resistance. They could reframe the transformation as an exciting chance to acquire new skills and create a more efficient, future-ready organization.

Hypothetical Examples and Hypothetical Case Studies

Example - Team Communication: A design team at a tech company was struggling with miscommunication and misunderstandings. The team leader, trained in NLP, introduced a system where each team member could express their communication preferences. By adapting to these preferences, the team significantly improved its communication and reduced misunderstandings, leading to more efficient work and better design outcomes.

Case Study - Organizational Transformation: A traditional manufacturing company needed to shift to a more sustainable production model but faced resistance from employees. They brought in an NLP coach who helped employees reframe this change as an exciting opportunity for personal growth and company survival in a changing market. The employees became more open to the change, and the transformation process was smoother and more successful than anticipated.

These hypothetical examples and hypothetical case studies illustrate how NLP can facilitate effective team building and organizational development, ultimately leading to improved performance and productivity.

How to Integrate NLP Techniques into Business Coaching

Integrating NLP techniques into business coaching involves understanding the client's needs, selecting appropriate NLP techniques, and customizing them for the client's context. It's also vital to ensure the client is comfortable with and understands the technique.

For instance, a business coach might use the 'Well-Formed Outcomes' technique with a client who struggles with goal-setting. The coach would explain the technique, guide the client through it, and help them refine their goals into well-formed outcomes.

Training and Certifying as an NLP Business Coach

Becoming an NLP business coach typically involves training in both business coaching principles and NLP techniques. Various organizations offer such training, some of which lead to certification. It's essential to choose a reputable training provider and to continue learning and practicing even after the training.

For example, an aspiring NLP business coach could take a course from an organization accredited by the International Coach Federation (ICF) and the American Board of NLP (ABNLP). After completing the course and passing an exam, they would receive certification and could then start practicing as an NLP business coach.

Challenges and Limitations of NLP in Business Coaching

While NLP can be very beneficial, it also has challenges and limitations. Not all NLP techniques work for everyone, and they require skill and sensitivity to apply effectively. Moreover, the scientific evidence supporting NLP is mixed, and it's essential to communicate this to clients.

One common challenge is client resistance or skepticism, especially given the mixed evidence base for NLP. Business coaches may need to address this by explaining what NLP is, providing examples of its effectiveness, and emphasizing that the client's experiences and perceptions will guide the coaching process.

Future Trends in NLP and Business Coaching

As business environments become more complex and challenging, there's likely to be increasing demand for tools like NLP that can enhance performance, communication, and resilience. At the same time, advances in technology and neuroscience might provide new insights into how NLP works and how to make it more effective.

For example, virtual reality (VR) technology might be used to enhance visualization techniques, allowing clients to immerse themselves in the situations they are visualizing. Moreover, advances in neuroscience could provide a deeper understanding of how NLP techniques influence brain processes, leading to the development of even more effective techniques.

Through these trends, the field of NLP and business coaching is likely to continue evolving, providing even more powerful tools for enhancing performance and productivity in the business world.

Hypothetical Case Study 1: Start-Up Business Development

Imagine a newly founded tech start-up struggling to pitch their product to potential investors. The founder, technologically adept but lacking sales experience, hires an NLP business coach. The coach applies 'Meta-Model' questioning to uncover the founder's limiting beliefs about sales and uses reframing to replace them with empowering beliefs. Next, they introduce mirroring and pacing techniques to help the founder build rapport with investors. As a result, the founder's pitching skills improve, leading to successful funding rounds.

Hypothetical Case Study 2: Leadership Coaching in a Large Corporation

Consider a newly promoted executive in a large corporation, tasked with leading a team of experienced professionals. Facing imposter syndrome and struggling with team leadership, they turn to an NLP business coach. The coach uses visualization and anchoring to help the executive see themselves as a capable leader and cultivate confidence. They also teach effective communication techniques like mirroring and pacing to foster rapport with the team. As a result, the executive becomes more confident, communication within the team improves, and the team's performance significantly increases.

Hypothetical Case Study 3: Team Building in a Medium-Sized Enterprise

Imagine a medium-sized enterprise facing low morale and lack of cohesion in one of their teams. The company hires an NLP business coach to facilitate team-building. The coach conducts workshops teaching the team NLP techniques like reframing for conflict resolution and mirroring and pacing for rapport building. The coach also facilitates open discussions where team members can express their communication preferences. As a result, team morale improves, communication becomes more effective, and the team becomes more cohesive and productive.

Hypothetical Case Study 4: Personal Productivity Coaching for C-level Executives

Suppose a C-level executive is struggling with time management and work-life balance, impacting their productivity and well-being. They engage an NLP business coach who introduces 'timeline therapy' to help the executive visualize tasks and manage their time more effectively. They also use the 'Swish Pattern' technique to help the executive manage stress and build resilience. As a result, the executive's time management improves, their stress levels decrease, and their overall productivity and well-being significantly enhance.

These hypothetical case studies illustrate the potential applications and benefits of NLP in business coaching. By providing practical tools for enhancing communication, mindset, leadership, team building, and productivity, NLP can significantly contribute to individual and organizational success in the business world.

Review of Key Points and Concepts

In this book, we've covered the principles of Neuro-Linguistic Programming (NLP) and its application in business coaching. We've delved into how NLP can facilitate mindset shifts, enhance communication, improve performance, foster team building, and facilitate organizational development. We've also discussed the process of implementing NLP into business coaching, including integrating techniques, training, and certification, and addressed the challenges and limitations of NLP.

The Impact and Importance of NLP in Business Coaching

NLP, when properly applied, can significantly contribute to business coaching's effectiveness. It provides practical tools for identifying and changing limiting beliefs, setting and achieving goals, improving communication, managing stress, enhancing leadership qualities, and boosting productivity. Moreover, NLP can help build trust and cohesion in teams and facilitate successful organizational change and development.

Closing Thoughts and Encouragement for Further Study and Application

While this book provides a comprehensive introduction to NLP in business coaching, there is much more to explore and learn. As with any skill, mastering NLP requires study, practice, and ongoing learning. Whether you're a business coach seeking to enhance your coaching effectiveness, a business leader aiming to improve your performance and leadership qualities, or someone interested in personal development, NLP offers valuable tools and techniques.

Additionally, as our understanding of the brain and human behavior evolves and as new technologies emerge, NLP is likely to continue evolving and diversifying. Therefore, I encourage you to keep learning, practicing, and staying open to new developments in the field.

By understanding and applying NLP in your business coaching practice or personal development journey, you can enhance your ability to communicate, influence, set and achieve goals, manage stress, lead effectively, and much more. Here's to your journey of discovery and growth with NLP!

Rex Morton is a renowned author and researcher in the United Kingdom with a passionate interest in the human mind, specifically in Cognitive Behavioural Therapy (CBT) and Neuro-Linguistic Programming (NLP).

Morton has spent a considerable portion of his professional life diving deep into the theories and principles that form the backbone of these two compelling fields. His fascination with NLP led him to complete an extensive certification program, solidifying his understanding of this innovative approach to understanding human behaviour.

Although Morton does not have clinical experience, his intense curiosity and dedication to studying these subjects have made him a respected figure in the field. He has thoroughly researched the integration of NLP techniques into CBT, offering fresh perspectives and insights into how these two methodologies can complement each other to enhance understanding of human cognition and behaviour.

As an author, Morton has successfully communicated his knowledge and passion to a broader audience, making complex psychological theories accessible to professionals and interested laypersons. His writing is characterized by a clear, engaging style and a focus on the practical application of theories, making them relevant to everyday life.

In his personal life, Morton is an ardent lover of the natural world, often spending his free time exploring the British countryside. His passion for landscape photography allows him to capture and share the beauty of these excursions. Despite his accomplishments, Morton is known for his humility and eagerness to continue learning. His work continues to inspire those interested in the intricate workings of the human mind and the exciting possibilities presented by the integration of NLP and CBT.

If you've found the content of this book enlightening and wish to continue your journey of understanding the human mind, I warmly invite you to visit my website at www.rexmorton.com. The website serves as a hub of knowledge where I share my latest findings, thoughts, and insights on the integration of NLP and CBT.

I also encourage you to subscribe to the newsletter available on the website. By subscribing, you'll receive regular updates on a range of topics, from detailed discussions on specific NLP techniques and their application in CBT, to the latest research in the field.

The newsletter is also the first place I'll share news of upcoming releases. Whether it's the announcement of a new book, the launch of an online course, newsletter subscribers will be the first to know. This is a great opportunity to continue learning directly from me, deepening your understanding of NLP and CBT, and enhancing your skills in applying these techniques in your own life or professional practice.

I'm looking forward to sharing this journey with you.